QUAKE
Built from Nothing

Pavement Poetry

Poems 'caught' during StAnza 2010
In an unofficial one-man fringe event

PoemCatcher Creations
Inspiration on the fly
St Andrew's, Scotland

www.poemcatcher.com
inspiration@poemcatcher.com
www.facebook.com : PoemCatcher

Published by PoemCatcher Creations
Salisbury Centre
2 Salisbury Centre
Edinburgh, EH16 5AB

www.poemcatcher.com

Copyright
All the poems in this book were donated.
The cover photograph was donated by Gillian

It would be thievery to steal the copyright from the authors themselves. It remains their own.
This is their beautiful creativity and I am just a creative collator.

Use of this material is welcomed – providing it inspires, engages and enthrals audiences.
Each and every poem in this book is brilliant. If you disagree, send £10 with your complaint to a child in Haiti.

This is a 3rd edition
The first 100 sold out in 3 weeks,
barely leaving enough for the charity launch

This is the 1st edition with an ISBN number.
Now we know it's a real book.
ISBN 978-0-9566018-0-3
Be proud to own it!

Excellent toilet reading
Best before: 04/2011
Do not refrigerate.

"He boldly and brazenly asked poets to write poems for him
For an anthology that he planned to print and sell at the festival
Where he was not famous, not a feature
A stylish vagabond from the fringe..."

From "The thief of Fife"
By John Akpata, Canadian performance poet

"Andrew's initiative in encouraging people to write poems and his intention to raise money for charity, is something to be applauded. We wish him luck with his project."

Eleanor Livingstone, Artistic Director, StAnza:
Scotland's International Poetry Festival

'A wonderful collection of poetry which mirrors the inner thoughts of a vast cross section of society'.

Provost Stephanie Young of East Ayrshire Council

Charity update

50 of the first 100 books were donated to SOS Children's Villages, raising £500.

The other 50 were sold privately and raised enough to print this second edition.

£3 from every book continues to go directly to Haiti's children.

Registered Charity Number 1069204

1 crazy idea...

4 days of begging for poems
139 fresh poems donated
7 languages

2 photos donated
(1 became the front cover)

21 books sold in 4 hours (pre-print)
100 books printed in 3 weeks

79 copies still for sale
Proceeds to charity
Send £10.

Contents

A personal note about this crazy project 1
Apologies (from you to me) 2
DAY 1: QUAKE 4
    Yeatsian Andour 4
    Rasim Valdes-laribi 4
    The Duel 5
    Quake : Limerick 6
    Unaffected 6
    Tremor 6
    Need 7
    Q.U.A.K.E. 7
    Old Course Shake 9
    Nearly 9
    Truth and Beauty 10
    Streetway 10
    Code poem for the French resistance 10
    Atlas 11
    Cannae Wriet 11
    Blighty 12
    Plea 12
    Quake 13
    Below 15
    Bite size writing 15

Everything fell over 15
Lost or found 16
Finding a place to beg 17
Climb 17
Musings on the Dire Wolf skeleton 18
Slippery 18
Intimate 18
Untitled dictation 19
A PoemCatcher observation 19
How to begin 20
Rhythm and rhyme 20
Cornering 21
Fresh pain 22
Shook 22
Confidence 23
Cry 23
Wave 24
Q 24
Visitors 24
Stable 25
Instructions 25
Blank 26
Quake Shake 26
Happy thoughts 26

Wobbles 27
Sexxxy Quake 27
Late Dawn 28
Exam quake 28
Gratitude 29
T-REX 30
Perspective 30
Ache 31
To quake for a Quaker 31
The Way of Seeing 32
Vanity 32
Quake 33
Critical 34
Doors 35

DAY 2: TIME 38
Poem for the man on the bench outside the Byre 38
Except when it doesn't 39
Tide 39
Time 40
Time 40
Contemplation – Saturday morning 41
Honouring 41
Time with nature 42
Time – the terror 44

Time for lunch 45

Commodity 46

Slipping by 47

Kavenaugh 1 48

Kavenaugh 2 48

Memories 49

Give time 49

Lost Time 50

Education 50

Anywhere 51

Nonsense 51

Mist 52

Windy Infinity 52

Sounds like time 53

"At the drop of a hat, like that" 53

Student time 54

Chance meeting 54

Taking advantage of the sun. 55

Element 55

The thief of Fife 56

Time 57

About intimacy… 58

untitled 58

Busy 58

Asking for Time 59

Trees 59

Goodbye 60

The most profound magnetic poetry 61

The Bench 62

Today's bench... 63

Equinox 63

By Colin Fraser 63

Cherry tree blossoms on the east coast 64

BYRE 65

My position 66

Time is an ocean 66

A poem about time.. 67

DAY 3: SOUL... 70

Soul; Sole; Sol 70

Sole 70

Devoid.. 70

Uhm, Sure 71

Soul 71

Poem for a young mother 72

Soul's for sale.. 72

Prayer 73

Spirit 74

Snowdrops 74

- Going Solo 75
- Spoken 76
- Everlasting 76
- Winter Sun 77
- "I've seen it twice" 78
- The Fish 78
- Collecting Poems 79
- Soul Karma 79
- If it was only the soul 80
- The Sole's Soul 81
- Miracle of … 82
- Cubical 83

DAY 4 : HAPPINESS 86
- Home sweet home 86
- Snowflakes 86
- Takeaway 87
- A random words poem by Chloe 88
- You're starting to look rubbish 89
- I remember happiness 90
- Ouch# 91
- breath 91
- After the Beatles 91
- 20 Words 91
- High Queues 92

Poemcatcher.. 93

A personal note about this project

In my therapy practice, I spend time helping people find their vitality; the places in their lives that bring them pleasure and step them towards health.

> **Creative places are always wrapped in pleasure, its simply divine.**

This poem-catching project has all the ingredients of every dream.

> *The idea; the growing internal detail; the doubt; the fear; the uncertainty; the courage; the trust; the action; the leap of faith; the realisations of the obvious; the moments of sheer stupidity; the 'aha' moments; the perfectly unplanned change of direction; the trashy bits; the lost and found; the success ; the reflection and reward of completion.*

So does each and every poem in this book.

It has been a privilege to watch you write, create and journey through your 'creative ingredients' on a pavement and a park bench.

I have one wish...

> **Please Believe.**
> **Believe in yourself.**
> **Believe in your creativity.**   **Its beautiful.**

Apologies (from you to me)

Dear PoemCatcher

Sorry for the handwriting that you could not read, and sorry for the metric rhythm that you could not follow and sorry for not giving the poem a title, and thank you, so much for giving it a title for me (why didn't you just ask?, I would have done it happily) and I forgive you for typing up the most poignant moment of the poem with the wrong word. (I promise to write neater next time).

Oh, don't worry about the auto-capitalising of all the little-letters I so carefully choose to punctuate. I understand the nuances of word-processing in a hurry.

Lastly sorry for not seeing my own brilliance. I wrote a great poem and then dissed it myself. I've had time to reflect and I'm pretty chuffed that I could write such an amazing poem so spontaneously. I really like my own poem. I was brilliant.

I promise to write some more

With Love
The Aspirational Poet

QUAKE

DAY 1: QUAKE

Yeatsian Andour

Poetry – how does one write a poem? Can one be written off the cuff? Yeats says that they are harder to write than many other works, but when a man implores you off the street to write something for a good cause, then although there is no time to dwell and work with yeatsian andour, yet hopefully the good will in these few lines will compensate for its rushed lack of poetry.

Anon.

Rasim Valdes-laribi

'damn the quake'
Say the slick, oiled, anchors
And their pundits in their shadows
'Damn all of them to hell'
Say their economic policy
Suits and opportunity,
The Market can't rebuild.

The Duel

We waited...
We waited on the outskirts
On the outskirts of town,
Waiting for the sun to rise
Watching as the birds forsook their nests
Wondering
What would happen to us next.
As we knew only one of us would return to the crowd
    and say
Which one had not survived the start of the day.

And the duel, which began
With a word and ended
With a bang
Waited
And waited.
For the quake of our foots,
The feat of our hearts
to still while the sun rose

  By Marissa Smit

Quake : Limerick

There once was a man called Blake
Who tried to snack on a snake
Bit its really quite hard
To catch a snake off its guard
So he donated a poem, which had the word, Quake

Anon.

Unaffected

From a land unaffected by quakes
Never experienced the chaos of the Earth's shakes
Can't know of their blights
But pray they're alright
And wish for peace and calm for their sake

By Dan Re

Tremor

Quake a tremor in the ground
A new fresh wave of media
Is gathered at the sound.

Euan Dickson

Need

My hands quake
Because i need
more coffee!

By Peggy

Q.U.A.K.E.

Quivering the earth begins to move
Under the ground a monster roars
Around the corner someone screams
Katastrophic!
Everything, everyone, everywhere.

By Deano

سکوت سرشار از ناگفته هاست
از جنبش‌ها، از گله‌ها، از آه‌ها، از دردها

 افراد پر عشق اگر لب به تکلم نگشایند
در دل کلمات حقیقت نهفته است

حقیقت قدس

Dr. P. Khosrow jah

Old Course Shake

St Paddy's Day
I awake
Stroll to the Old Course
Looking to play with others
A good game and good verse
First off the tee
7a.m.I hit a great shot
A thundering quake.

By Derek McKinnon
Nova Scotia, Canada

Nearly

Wanting nothing but your ears
And rhymes of those who dares
Inspiration to let flow
Instead I get your "NO"
AND GLARES AND STARES
AND NOSTRIL FLARES
And even less
From plugged in ears
Thank goodness for those who care
And dare
To meet my stare
(and be inspired)

By Andrew Newman

Truth and Beauty

Beauty and truth

By Simon C

Streetway

Stopped streetway by a
Church and some flowers
And a mild hat
To include a minute-long
'quake' of half-thought
To a pebbled face
Into a hal-sunny day
For somebody, windily

By Aisha Fair

Code poem for the French resistance

The life I have
 Is all that I have,
And the life that I have is yours.
The Love that I have
  Of the life that I have
    Is yours and yours and yours.

Fondly carried by Patricia.

Atlas

Brute Poseidon's insatiable wrath
Spares no ship from tempest's path
Argosie nor Spanish galleon
Can halt the ocean's black battalion

Nor shall mortal tools or toils
Save our land-borne empires girth
Should Altas shrug, he'll strew the oils,
And stormy Quake shall drown the earth.

By Gavin Willow

Cannae Wriet

The effects of an earthquake
Shock, horror and the shake
Hope is and enduring concept
But an essentiality too
My poetic creativity is poor
But not as poor as those affected by the quake
Believe, have faith and hope
And with good fortune you will cope.

By Charlie

(Who professed poor ability to so many times that I was truly surprised that he stopped and "gave it a go". Well done Charlie.)

Blighty

Tainted by the dust
From someone else's disaster
I stand apart, watching
Around me broken glass, broken buildings
Broken lives.

Carefully imported, our sandwiches,
Wrapped in cellophane, are dust free.
Our technology, black and shining,
Shockingly whole in this
Shattered world,
Record, records, records,
So that home, on their sofas,
They may sigh.

By Margaret McDonald

Plea

Today please think of a child's
fate
Of the pain and turmoil of an
Earthquake

By Clarissa Whileholn

Quake

On a whim I went to St. Rules
To gaze at the great eyeless walls
That gaze themselves out to the sea
And seem to stare back at me.

I saw a slate that was a floor
Raised in the cathedral, years before,
And beneath wee coffins where the dead
Were gently placed, trunk and head

Laid in a carved casket, to the shape
Of skull and shoulders, back and nape;
What is it, I thought, to lie,
How does it feel, I thought , to die?

The thing about the ruined pile
Is its silence, all the while
Looking like a recent site [as stones break]
The locus of an ancient quake

I thought this as I stepped inside
The coffin, where I lay, and tried
To imagine the walls coming down
On history without a sound.

By Jay Bernard

Soarele încă se ascunde
Dar o să-l caut
Până o să cad obosită
Până când nu o să mai
 simt picioarele
"Oare" ce e asta?
"Poate trebui să îmi crească
 aripi
Poate trebui să mă
 topesc
"Oare" unde e locul
 ăsta?
O să-l caut și o să-l
 găsesc
Într-o altă contopire
Într-o altă poezie.

 Georgiana

Below

Ripples in the lake,
The grand beneath shakes
   Oh shit,
It is an Earthquake

Anon.

Bite size writing

This is how the cookie crumbles
  Filling up the tummy rumbles
    Words flow from the falling crumbs
      And line by line a poem becomes
        The verse devoured in mouthful glee
          The poem, the pen in ecstasy.

By Andrew Newman

Everything fell over

This headache is bad, I'm overhung
I shouldn't have danced, I shouldn't have sung
Dundee was only a good idea
After way too much wine and way too much beer.
My head is spinning
My stomach 's not winning
My Head, My head
Back to bed.

By Angela

Lost or found

The young man, a student probably,
Called out to me as I
Emerged from the narrow wynd
Feeling my way around the town.

He was sat on the pavement
Youthful dark hair, t-shirt and jeans
Cheeky twinkles in his eyes
Inviting.

"Free poetry" he calls
Or was it "fresh poetry"/
Anyway,
Something that suggests recent writing
He called to me,
I must look like a poet
Or lost.
A lost poet, looking for a place to write,
To edit, to log observations
Thoughts and ideas.

I nodded acknowledgement
And walked on
As if I should know
Where I was going.

By Louise Grisoni

Finding a place to beg

The church bells tolled
The place to sit
The sun's shine shone
An angel's fit
Divine inspired and crazy too
The vision, poems are coming through.
Just write and trust
The words will be
Expressions of
Cre-A-tive-ity

By the PoemCatcher

Climb

Quake- A shiver, a tremble
A movement within me, the cause inknown.
I ignore it at first but it rolls on harder
Oscillating my every bone,
My joints and organs rattle
Harder, louder, stronger
No breath to fight with
Then
Stop.

By the ice pick guy.

Musings on the Dire Wolf skeleton

(At the Page Museum of Los Angeles...)

You alas are extinct
And cannot come out to play.

By Devon Moody.

Slippery

Nothing makes me quake
Like a slimy big black snake

By Kate Hofstra

Intimate

I quake I tremble
I fall
And it was good
You were good

By Sophia Blue-eyes. X.

Untitled dictation

    There was an earthquake
        One fine day
    There was a sound
        It burst away

    Then it was quiet
        There was no sound
           The everything
        Suddenly
           Fell to the ground
    Death all around.

    Not a loving soul.
    All covered up
    In a great big hole.

Dictated by the guy with the awesome hat and uber-beard, affectionately described as an "old Geezer"

A PoemCatcher observation

    "I have no time
    I'm in a rush"

    Shouldn't you be running?

How to begin

I don't even know where to start,
Words and feelings - should they come from the heart?
Or should I write of daffodils and polar bears?
Or raindrops that catch me unawares?
I don't even know how to begin
Beginning implies something you imagine
Or badly rhymed and strung together
Linking words on the street forever.

By Jenny

Rhythm and rhyme

Rhythm in poetry for me is a must
Without it the poetry doesn't seem just
And rhyme with the rhythm it too sounds fine
Give me rhythm in poetry, rhythm and rhyme

By Rosalind Gerton

Cornering

Sitting on the street
Waiting for people to meet
He asked me for a poem
And at first I thought him gnome
But I said yes
And I had to guess
About where to rest my case
So it would not be taken
It really made me quake.
That's it.
My whole bit.

By one of the Andrew Young's

(yup there were two,
And though not together,
not far apart ,
and I wonder how
the parents did start,
and choose such a name
to couple insane
co-incident
on this street corner)

Fresh pain

A call came through and shook me awake
I thought my world was safe from quakes
But alas not so for life was fake
S o here I am too wide awake
With a pain in my heart that has left
Very wide awake.

By Yaganoma Baatuolkuu

Shook

Pictures hang skew now
  On walls cracked
Sunday's tea cups
Lay shattered below the
  Place of neatness
Where prim and proper
Display the family silverware
And best of all
NO-ONE CARES.
Gratitude has burst in the lives
Dulled by familiarity
   Day-in day-out sameness
Flushed away.
  Thank goodness
 For the quake

By Andrew Newman

Confidence

Everyone say's "its bad"
The words that MAKE ME MAD
That cre-a-tiv-ity
  Finds no place to be
    Admired
      Once set free

A PoemCatcher observation

Everyone says "they can't" or "its no good".
I praise the possibility
of ability
emergent
fresh.

Cry

They watched the buildings crumble
And cried "For heaven's sake"
This really can't be normal
It must be an earth quake

By Del Jones

Wave

Quake a dreadful wave beneath the ground
A wave of ruin, a crashing sound
A simple word with dreadful connotations
A terrible event that can and will destroy nations
Quake a dreadful wave beneath the ground
A wave of ruin, a final sound.

By Evan Dickson

Q

Q uirky
U nderdogs
A scertain
K evorkian
E rudition.

Visitors

Scotland is like a quake
Hitting us with beauty
History abounds
Deep within its grounds
We'll be back again...

By Erica Strowbridge
(From Nova Scotia)

Stable

Yesterday life was stable
Then something happened
Underground the earth moved
People above quaked in the houses

By Josef Anton

Instructions

Walking through St Andrew's
Meeting a guy
Asked for my help
A poem from I
To include the word quake
The challenge is set
Here is my poem
....
"Damn" no rhyme yet
...
And so we are done
The challenge is met

By Solvoterra

Blank

Nothing in my head today
St Patrick's took it all away
Guinnessed by the brothy stout
That's left me here
My head without
A thought, a word or poem to pen
    I'll give up
        This is the end.

Inspired by Jessica's hangover

Quake Shake

Quake Shake the trees shake in the
Quake houses fall in the quake but roses
Bloom in the quake and that's not fake
And for god's sake help those who have fallen in the quake

By The other Andrew Young

Happy thoughts

Quake here, Quake there
Quakes are everywhere
Take them quakes away
And make it a happy day

By Max Rath

Wobbles

Poem, poem, poem, poem, poem, poem...
I don't know how to write good prose, so here goes.

Come and quake and sit and
Sing , tomorrow we can
Quake together from here
Can see myself a reflection
Everyday and when I look
It quakes

By Anyusha Rose

Sexxxy Quake

Lets spin yr socks
In this ol' tumble dryer
Lets lean against it, baby
And feel the quake

By R.V.W

Late Dawn

Today did not dawn
This is the horror I know
Streetlights on past 10 am
Warm feet, cold floors, hot tea
Knees quake as I contemplate
Steep climbs into academic perches
This is the horror I know
The only horror.
Paper delivery offers transport to another world
Escapism tempts, headlines scream
QUAKE!
I don't know this horror
I walk away from the paper
And the trash can
And the cosy comforts of a house
That still stands.

By H.M.R.

Exam quake

Exams make me in my shoes Quake
They're stressful and nasty , for goodness sake
I'd rather spend my time baking a cake
Or working in the garden
With a rake.

By David Clark

Gratitude

We stopped in our tracks
To avoid giant cracks
Where buildings had toppled
Onto their backs

People were crying
While others were dying
Scattered around
bodies are lying

So what could we do
For goodness sake
We'd landed in the middle
Of a monstrous quake
So dig deep in your pockets
And the rubble too
To help these poor people through,
And just thank God
It wasn't you.

By the toilet attendant

T-REX

It was 1993 when a T-rex
First appeared on my TV

The way the ground shook
Under that big scaley foot
Made me squeal and hide
(I was 5 and totally petrified)
But this is now and that was then
Its 17 years later in 2010

And now "Quake" always reminds me
Of how Jurassic Park came to Haiti.

By Kirsty Alexander

Perspective

Did the earth move for you?
(Yes, but not in the way you think)
To get a perspective on anything
Move your position and take
A better point of view.

By Kevin Cadwallender

Ache

What was that ache?
My heart started to quake
The whole world, my bones started to shake
And now I feel really quite feint

By Amarkel Dessain

To quake for a Quaker

Quake, built from nothing
With soul-striving
Fox would nod his silent
              Approval
A moment of stillness
    In busyness
    Between poets quests

By Derek Read

The Way of Seeing

To imaginatively break the grammar – (and time)
Rules for appearances the most matter-real
And perfect incarnations of partical philosophy
Is always. A typewriter making the clay vase quake
On the table, its pinkribbon is
The proven best colourtouch, is
Neverless the
Order of the eye that holds, references
And modifies its own dativity.

By Calum Gardner

Vanity

Vanity – a poet's undoing
She says. I quake, hearing
That truth. For Vanity
Takes many form, not least
A fake humility.
My Catholic conscience accuses me.
Oh, to be open as a book
On whose blank leaves
Words drop out of the air
Settle themselves like birds
Tired from a flights
Against the wind.

Anon.

Quake

The tenacity
of these pearly, ethereal
lanterns
seems impossible for a thing
of living glasswork,
forged in the protective soil
from which it now emerges--
a small, persistent snowdrop.
Like so many who have faced
the threat of devastation,
it faces the cold wind, trembling.
Brave snowdrop!
You quake in the face
of the unknown,
yet your glittering bell
sings an unheard melody
which, if perceived,
is a herald of the end
of an age of ice,
and a reassurance
that though you shiver,
your roots have held you fast
past threat
into a ringing dawn.

By Sabrina Russo

Critical

They write up my lines
split me into chapters
catalogue my references
print the whole works
get me in the bookshops
bad-mouth me in print
& I
haven't
even
opened my
mouth :
yet !

*

تأويل

يملونني سطوراً
فصولاً ويبوبونني
ثم يفهرسونني
ويطبعونني كاملاً
المكتباتِ ويوزعونني على
ويشتمونني في الجرائدِ
وأنا
لمْ
أفتحْ
فمي
بعد

Doors

I rap on a door
It opens up
All I see of the door is me !
It opens up
Through I go
Nothing but another door.
Lord how many more
Holding myself back from me ?

*

أبواب

أطرقُ باباً
أفتحهُ
إلا نفسي باباً لا أبصر
أفتحهُ
أدخلُ
لا شيء سوى بابٍ آخر
يا ربي
يفصلني عني كمْ باباً

By: Adnan al-Sayegh
عدنان الصائغ

Translated by Stephen Watts and Marga Burgui-Artajo

36

TIME

Then	went	tick	forward
When	was	tock	backward
Late	when	later	yet
Soon	would	now	
Early	were	rush	

DAY 2: TIME

Poem for the man on the bench outside the Byre

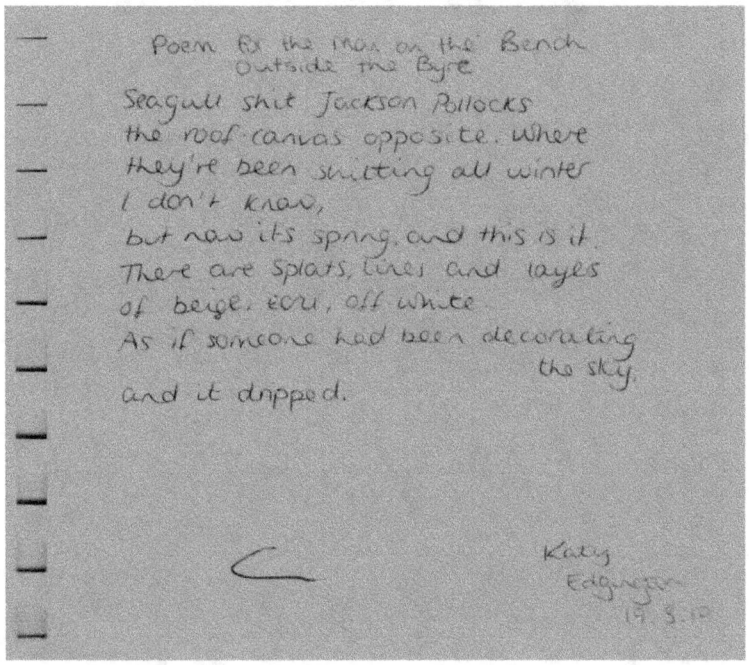

Poem for the man on the Bench
Outside the Byre
Seagull shit Jackson Pollocks
the roof canvas opposite. Where
they're been shitting all winter
I don't know,
but now its spring, and this is it.
There are splats, lines and layers
of beige, ecru, off white
As if someone had been decorating
the sky,
and it dripped.

Katy
Edgington
19.5.18

Except when it doesn't

I like poems that rhyme / all the time
Except the last line / when it doesn't

A contrasting end / I recommend
To send / your spirit soaring

Verse that is blank / is rank
So no thank / you can keep it

On the other hand / there's some demand
For it to be banned / yeh but I think

Those who prefer it / merit
A ferret / up their trousers

'cause I like poems that rhyme / all the time
Except the last line / when it doesn't.

By Helen McFadden

Tide

The tide inks blackness
Bordered on the edge by extinguished gloom
Hopes (these frail night sprats)
That silver minnon, on the shore
Show a seapath with traveler on beyond
Could this just be a pointer
To quite another land?

By Avril Martin.

Time

T ime
I s
M eaningless
E nough

By M. Fitz

Time

Time hangs behind

Time runs ahead

Time is hungry.

By Chipper Scott

Contemplation – Saturday morning

The sun shining
The cool caress of the breeze
The shriek of the maws
Remind me of you
Of times past
Perhaps of times to come
All is possible within
The kaleidoscope of life

By Andrea Tilney

Honouring

I met a man today who collects
Pieces of people's Souls
He wasn't a demon with cloven feet
And he didn't shine like an Angel
He was just a man on a park bench
Who smiled, and asked if I'd like
To give a part of myself to him.
I laughed, and even stranger,
I could not wait to do so.

By the man with the ponytail in passing

Time with nature

　　She tells me her endless abundance of time will await you forever more,
　　She tells me this when we converse on a windy beach, mountain top of moor
　　Our meeting place does not matter – my conclusions are always the same,
　　Spending time with nature brings nothing but delight, fascination and gain.

　　I will tell my children that forever can be held within their hands – it can be found within a single seed,
　　And as the seeds blow from the dandelion, millions of years combine to give a plant all she will need,
　　Upon settling down, she will rise up tall and into life make her way,
　　Perhaps she will achieve and Oak's hundred years, perhaps a flowers pollination chances in just a single day.

　　We are together as one within this world, all of life is made of the same,
　　We are far from separated from the past – it lives within our soil, it lives within our bones
　　It is found within our prized possessions, even the building blocks of our homes

　　Time is endless but all too often we think, in this form, not so are we,
　　Perhaps this is why we run around with watches, striving endlessly from time to be free,
　　But settle down a while, find yourself alone but within nature not disconnected,

Life goes on in the simple things, it lives on in ways most unexpected.

When I join the earth and leave behind my children, I will tell them not to feel alone
I will tell them to head to the mountains and I will encourage them to roam,
They will see the rocks, they will feel the wind and they will become re-connected,
With the fabric of life which unites us all and they will realize they are not as alone as perhaps they first ~~expected~~ suspected

Kindest wishes, Gillian.
(who also donated the cover photo)

Time – the terror

What a terror time is
How he makes us down
(No escape in country
No escape in town)

Turns the dancing children
Into weary wives
Then to sad old turtles
Then he takes their lives.

In the nightmare darkness
Somewhere after one
Of the horror of it –
All that he has done.

By Deidre Barrie

Time for lunch

Snuggling on the hotplate
To the side of
Spectacular vanilla follies
In a spotlight with coffee towers at £1.35
An onion bridie and a pie
Bleeding grease

Tucked into two paper bags
I munch them on the
Way up the road
Into the wind

Grease on the paper
And my fingers
And the poem.

By Elspeth Mclean (with edits!

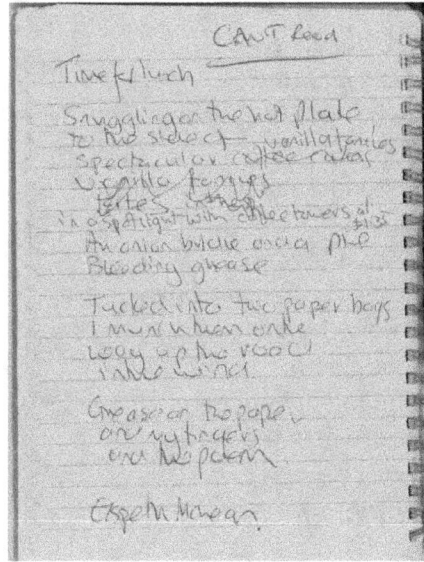

Commodity

He's here to lard up, isn't he,
Lay on thick wads of fat
Finish up the scraps
Fill his skin; do his bit
Until the abattoir
The black shriek, the slit throat,
Spilt shambles on the floor;
To swing from the hook, to drip
On dust, await the dreamer's thud
As it sings the bone.

We're here to salt the bellies,
Make bacon, freeze the meat
Trade the stocks, fatten the wallet
On the bristling back of it.
As we run hither and thither-
Packing room to freezing shed
To trading floor, his blood
On our feed, deadline met-
The pig wins every time.
He knows what he always knew.

Life is to sleep in a square of sunlight
To scratch the bristles
Against the splintery post,
Push out a belly grunt, to trough.
No matter how short the life,
How grim the death.
It's only the time in between
That makes it worth the crack

By C. Daventry

Slipping by

Slipping by
Rushing past
Lost again
Found at last

See it on the faces before you
Always starting
Never ending
Take care to cherish this beautiful blending

By Claudia Olivie

Kavenaugh 1

Time for reflection
No time to write
It can't be kavenaugh, but still exciting
A stanza's gone, a lifetime past
The very first verse, perhaps the last

Written by a self-skeptic.
Who knew for sure he had no ability,
But slowed down enough to start,
To simply tell me what he saw.

He came back later with a second version
For which I truly thank him.

You alone have the talent to convince
Those who believe they can't,
doubt they can
or devalue their own attempts.

Your evolving poems are the very reason for starting.
You are the reason for this project.
Keep writing.

Kavenaugh 2

St Patrick's Day has barely passed and Kavenaugh
In quiet contemplation, sits cloistered in St Andrew's
His hat reflective, he reflecting, in vain for Liffey water
waiting
But still the spirit of Powers Lingers

Memories

'Tis due to pidgeons that alight
  On Nelson's hat
    That makes it white.

By Spike Mulligan,
Carried fondly by Bill.

Give time

Take the time
To give a smile
To a friend or a stranger
Take the time
For someone else
You will feel loved and blessed
And last of all take the time for you
Even if it's just sitting
Reading
Winnie the Pooh

By Stephanie Young
Provost East Ayrshire Council

Lost Time

Tick,...
Look it's gone, hiding
  I'll search and when I've
    Found it's face, I'll tock to you.

By 'someone' Buchan Cameron
With apologies for not being able to read your first name!

Education

Time teaches love
Love teaches pain
This evening passes like every other
Sheherazade's hour is swift
But my wait is long

By J.A.

Anywhere

If I'm going nowhere
Then I hope it's better there
Than anywhere I might have found
If I had dared to look around
If I asked directions
I would only see connections
From the path I travel, sometime blind
To other paths I left behind
But if I choose to go
Down the path I do not know
Then eventually I'll end up there
In that elusive place "somewhere"

By Susannah Peel

Nonsense

I'd like to be no-nonsense,
But why the big pretense?
If there wasn't any nonsense
Then where would be the sense?

By Susannah Peel

Mist

The mist in haste escaping from the sea
Like a convict finding itself free
Came creeping through the town without a sound,
And not a dewy footprint on the ground
Then moving on it vanished out of sight
But I was witness to it's silent flight

By Susannah Peel

Windy Infinity

The seconds of sun
  Drift off with the gales
    Dreams disappear with the morn
      Favoured fantasies fall down the well.

By Carly Matthews

Sounds like time

Church bells fill the vacantness
The silence rings around
Time echoes though the alleyways
Expressed in joyful sound

By Andrew Newman

"At the drop of a hat, like that"

Sunny morning, beautiful day
Sitting on bench, not much to say
    Clock ticks on
    Clock ticks on
Today it's here
Tomorrow it's gone.

By Moira

Student time

> Biological Deadlines
> 1. Lab report
> 2. Essay
> 3. Application
>
> A. Pollination cycles
> B. Is there enough time to fix the damage
> C. Planning for the future
>
> Guess I better start.

Inspired by G.

Chance meeting

I took a walk on windy March day
Met two beautiful people on the way
They sat together on a bench by the Byre
Encouraging passers by a little poetry to inspire
I'm glad I took the time.

By Marjorie McFadjen

Taking advantage of the sun.

If it were possible
For sure, I'd try
To take advantage
    of the sun.

I'd catch and bottle
I'd tin and dry
To take advantage
    of the sun.

I'd bask and bake it
In a pie
To take advantage
    of the sun.

I'd sell for profit
Heal Scotland's cry
To take advantage
    Of the sun.

By Andrew Newman

Element

A son and a daughter
A word out of line
A fish out of water
A man out of time

By Michale Sked

The thief of Fife

In St. Andrew's I met a charming confident thief
A man named Andrew from Cape Town
Who arrived with a cap on his head
That hid the cap in his hand
He boldly and brazenly asked poets to write poems for him
For an anthology that he planned to print and sell at the festival
Where he was not famous, not a feature
A stylish vagabond from the fringe
Who unashamed and unabashed and unhindered
Bamboozled the bards into planting seeds in his yard
And he proudly sold their work back to them
And he proudly wallowed in his shamelessness
As he allowed the poets to create and donate
Their words, which are all stolen
And give to the thief of Fife
A man named Andrew who arrived in St. Andrew's
With a cap on his head
That hid the cap in his hand

By John Akpata

Time

    I have reached the
      time of life

When sunglasses play
   Hide and seek on your head
   Evading your search
   Through bag and pocket and case.
When lips lose their
   Bedroom pout like
   The ticking gone flat in the
   Duvet they once nestled under
When words go hiking
   In the hills, unable
   To find their way back
   From the valleys
   Of the cortex range
When one learns to
   hear such losses
   As a friends knocking

An old friend knocking

Or else make an
Enemy of time

I have reached the time of
Life to know the
Loss of that.

By Suzanne Zeedyk

About intimacy...

Truth is an
Unopened present
To be unwrapped
Only in the dark

By Kathleen Walker

untitled

The silence of betrayal
Of an unexploded bomb
The affirmation of a space
Where something should be.

By Kathleen Walker

Busy

Waiting outside for my mate
The wind is strong and its late
Time on my hands
So much I can't stand
I must flee from this clocktown!
Where everyones' busy
I have got time
But everyones' too busy to have some of it.

By Marcus Ker

Asking for Time

You are already
Dead to me
Young man who
Asks of time
I see the flowering
Of aberrant cells
In your unaware flesh
A sludge accumulate
Your fresh beating heart

What things I have seen
Between this world and the next
Between where we are
And what is to come
It is an imagination
Of grieving
But wonder
But wonder

Autographed with illegible flair

Trees

The old Mulberry is dying
And already they have planted
A daughter tree back
Branched in March
Glued with the holm-oak's
Evergreen sheltering arm

By Anna Crowe
(With possible errors in translation)

Goodbye

Across the stubbled field
   She ran
Eyes wide in childish
         wonderment
And as she ran she waved
A blood red hankerchief
Her father's
Towards the distant figure
       on the hill
And as she ran she cried
 They lied
   They lied
 He did not die
And glanced again
Towards the empty hill
 And heard a voice
Or was it the whisper of
   the wind
A simple word.
   Goodbye.

By J.Y Young

The most profound magnetic poetry
ever found on a refrigerator in a university dorm room

"Why is time dark?"

By James fallen carried by Ryan Van Winkle

The Bench

Time was you loved this place
But time moves one
And now you are remembered on the poetry seat

By Helena Winnicka

Today's bench

Today's park bench is as rich
As yesterday's pavement
Blessed with time
I sat in aloneness
Trusting the day

By Andrew Newman

Equinox

To every thing there used to be a season
But seasons have been thrown into confusion
They're often indistinguishable now
Like those Vivaldi wrote into his music
After he'd met some Scottish summer weather

By Margaret Christie

By Colin Fraser

    It is easy to hide a rhyme
            Where rhythm should be

By Colin Fraser

Cherry tree blossoms on the east coast

A cherry tree blossoms on the east coast
Even though it is only March
And further south the branches clamped
Dumb dulcimers without the hammers of warm summer rain

On South street light chips
Hard as stones in your eyes
On North street the buds
Still rattle like black ribs against spring.

But in between
Walled in stones
The sun startles in the crocuses
Wind flashes across the upturned primroses
Testing their grip of the season
And above
Blazing a trail for summer
In North sea brazen pink
Deliberate on the ship
Of the stiff gale
A cherry tree blossoms on the east coast.

By Lise Sinclair

BYRE

The warmth o gressy braith
Haes lang syne tyned frae here.
Nae kye or owsen
Tether t in their stalls.
The place is thrang wi
Fremmit airty fowk,
Whaes craic an havers
Kittles up a warld,
O language, thocht an wirds
That binds us aa thegaither;
Instinctively this ither herd
Muives oan.

The warmth of grassy breath
Has long since left this place.
No cows or oxen tethered
In their stalls.
The place is thronged with
Strange, arty folk.
Whose talk and chat conjures
Up a world,
Of thought and language, words
That bind us all together;
Instinctively this other herd
Moves on.

By Rab Wilson.

My position

I've been here since it all began
I hope to be here, when it ends again
Kind of lost, Now, in between
What comes next is, what's to be seen

By Marosh Peterson

Time is an ocean

"Time is an ocean
but it ends at the shore"
sang Bob Dylan.
der in der Universität von St. Andrews
einen Ehrendoktortitel erhielt
Aus diesen Informationen
müsste sich doch ein Gedicht
machen lassen,
dachte ich...
Doch leider nicht.
                Andreas

A poem about time

A man on a park bench
Asked me to write a poem about time
At precisely the moment
I had carved one fat hour from the day
And my mind was already on the cliff path
Heading for the bay.

Already, I had to chose between
The challenge of the harbor wall
Straight as an exclamation mark
And the elyptical question of the bench

But I have just enough time
To notice how each gust of wind
Lifts a veil of sand
And scatters it, like ashes on eth waves.
How gulls are somersaulted like paper,
And two stately swans
Glide incongruously on the open sea.

A man tosses stones to his dog
Which loses them in the tide
But leaps and wags its tail
Laughing at its own ridiculousness.

This might be one of those St. Andrew's day's
The poet says we'll pay for
When the accounts are called in
But the thing about time is
It's not how you spend it
But the moments you hold it
And feel its weight

In the cup of your hands.

By Susan Mansfield

SOUL

My soul lifted
by the simple pleasure
of an unexpected smile

Elaine Hunter

DAY 3: SOUL

Soul; Sole; Sol

Fish; shoe; spirit
Alone; beer; sun

 Spirit
Fish Shoe alone
    Beer Sun

Sole

I am a happy Soul
And that is that

By Elly!

Devoid

Out of nothing
Towards nothing
In between : soul

By Ally J.G

Uhm, Sure

I'm not a poet,
But they tell stories
So I might actually fit,
Some soul in my bowl

By M Belk

Soul

Oh, Soul,
ankle-deep in the cold fast stream,
snow-melt soul,
where are you going?

soul unseen,
soul taking note of silence

Ah soul,
colour of Lebanon
colour of longing,
      Beautiful scarce longing –
are you on your way home?

Labouring soul,
anima alone, all alone,
crossing the cold fast stream...

By Penelope shuttle

Poem for a young mother

M is for mother, so tired and so grim
O is for other, who's making a din.
T is for Toffler, the queen of the world
H is for headache as empires unfold.
E is for easy – I'm sure it was once
R is for reeling at all of their wants
I is for something I try to recall
N is for no-one, just no-one at all
G is for gladness as bedtime comes near

S is for sleeping soon after beer
U is for underwear all round the floor
N is for no-one, just no-one at all.
D is for daily & desperate & dear
A is for always and wanting them near
Y - well, it's a good question.

By Mary Gunn

Soul's for sale

How much for a soul today?
Do you take credit, or do you ask for cash?
Perhaps the recent shortage of souls for sale
Tells us business of grosser kinds is on the mend.

By Ben Gutme

Prayer

I am not apathetic
I hate what happens in the world
Does it come from God
Or the devil
I often tell God – I hate you
And hear nothing but my own ...soul
I am not apathetic
But I do not give
I listen, am interested
Concerned for those ...foes
So sorry
But afterwards there is a house to clean
Dinner to make
Classes to pass
So I am not apathetic
Non-complacent, maybe
Does God mind?

By A.M.

Spirit

                     Soul

              -   invisible -

       heartbeat of a nation
           -   pulsing   -

       beyond destruction

By Angela Blacklock- Brown

Snowdrops

White drops
    Give way to blue silla
The body
    Gives way to the soul
All our promises
    Give way to God's
        Promise

By Paul Abdul Wadud

Going Solo

AH SAW
A SOUL
SOAR
WAY UP
OAN ITS AIN

By Hugh Bryden

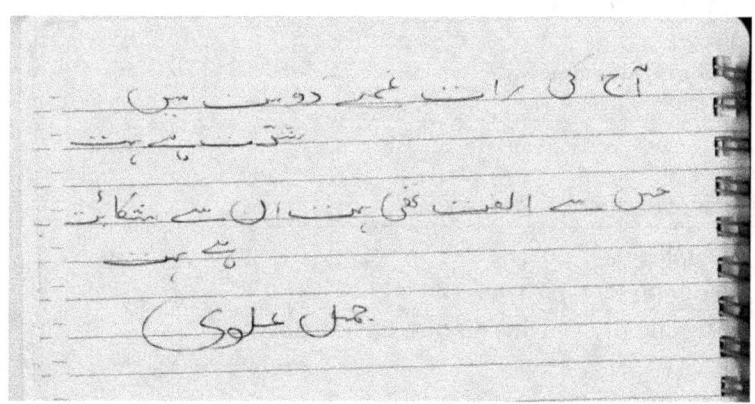

Spoken

The poet's voice
Echoes softness of soul
Dancing between words
And stanza's of rhyme
Depth arises through disorder
Dissolving barriers
Linguists built
O'er time.

Softness quakes
The ground we walk
Softness quakes
The ground we walk
Inspired to the sea

By Andrew Newman

Everlasting

Helpless,
Hopeless
Turning my soul inside out, upside down

Leaves me gasping for air

Your breath on my lips
Lips touching
Everlasting

By Thomas Crichton

Winter Sun

Our two souls
Entwined
As we walk
The winter beach
As soft grasses
Hush
And we melt
Into nothingness

By Rosie Summerton

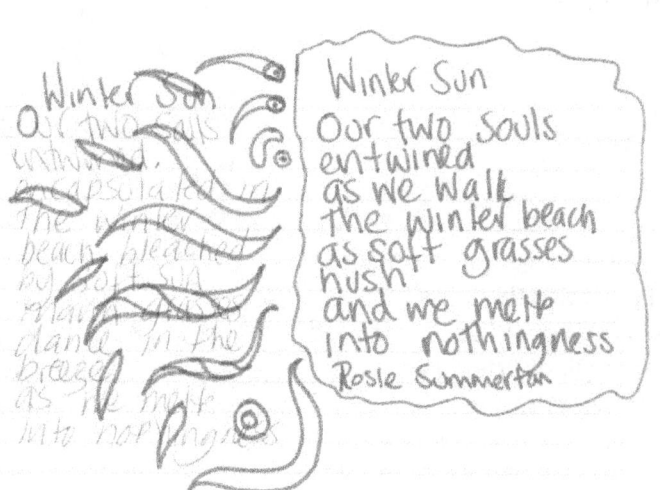

"I've seen it twice"

I've seen it twice
Once down under,
Once in my alma mater,
Rolling, rolling, rolling
The endless movement
Of water

I've heard it,
But only
In the poetry of others
And the moments you cannot describe

This
Is the sound of astounded souls.

By Andrew F.I. Duff

The Fish

My soul tells me not to drink
But I am a fish that
Needs the booze like water
So off to Oktoberfest I go
To slay zee germans.

By T.W.

Collecting Poems

(to the reader)

Being a participant
All I can say
Is the pleasure will be yours

By Jonathan Pryce

Soul Karma

I believe in life after death
I believe that life is breath

By Desne Masie

If it was only the soul

If it was only the soul
To emerge untarnished
Glistening with passage
Rather than time
That lines the face
Bends the back
Into unwilling torpor

This soul here
This child
So much of me
But not
Radiant with
Newness.

By Morgan Downie

The Sole's Soul

Caught on the hop
He asked for my soul
As I was on the hop
Examined my sole

No answer came
Too crowded
Too lost
Too footweary

My Soul has left
Me empty

StAnza's to reason

By J.E. Kille
For Chris Flint

Miracle of …

Miracle of красоты.

Я верю в чудеса
As strangers smiles alight
Живу и вижу их во всём
And then my world is bright

Ведь нет пределов красоте
And every day means living
Мне всё же не уйти от пустоты
And the world around forgiving.

М. Левитанус
L. Codding

Cubical

Standing in the dregs of human soup
A community of skin cells
Make a microscopic raft for bubbles

The shower water lifts
The bottles off their feet
And the confused school
Knudge each other
Paddle around your toes

Bodies clean and fleeting
Flicker through the glass
Don't even leave a shadow
of their soul

By Laila Sumpton

84

Happiness

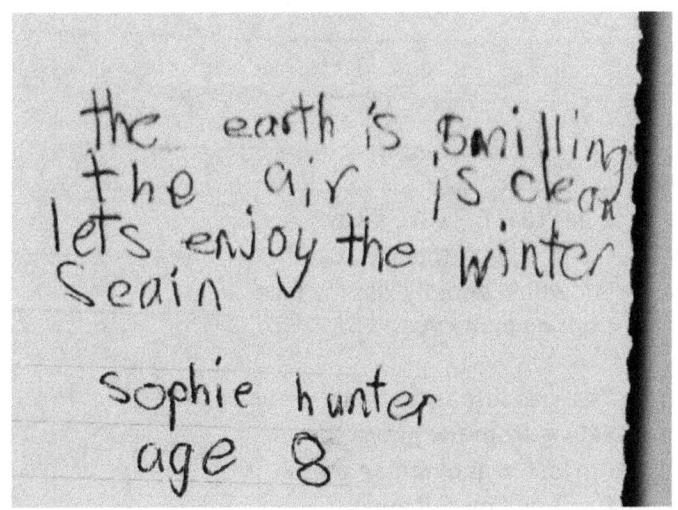

DAY 4 : HAPPINESS

Home sweet home

> Happiness resides
> In the time it takes
> To read these lines.
>
> A.K.

Snowflakes

> Can't tear my gaze away
> I'm staring at the sky
> Snowflakes coldly kiss my face
> Melting in my eyes
>
> Tears as soft as feathers
> Falling from the grey
> I'm lost in gaping-openness
> Can't pull myself away.
>
> With love from Rachel

Takeaway

We're eating chips with our fingers
Standing at the entrance to the lane
As the tiny-skirted girls shriek past
On a clear, dark night on the coast.
He keeps glancing down at me
While I tell him,
Plucking with fingers so smeared
I'll taste the salt for days,
Offering him my life
One chip at a time

By Tracey S. Rosenberg

A random words poem by Chloe

20 words were pulled from a paper in a "pen-meets-dartboard" style and the task set. The following poem emerged.

Rooney the Dishwasher browses the job section

Happiness for him was the happy situation
when he put down a dish and became a musician
for the bottom of the dish sung out a ringing recollection

of the morning mass of singing by the birds in his garden
who had been spending all their days asking God for his pardon.
(And by 'God' of course he meant the most Imperial Commander!)

It seemed the publicappointments published nothing but the danger
of a stirrup up to the rolling world of God-like 'changers'.
(And by 'God' of course he meant the most don't-talk-to type of stranger!)

By Chloe Morrish

Can you spot the 20 words? See the poem titled "20 Words"

You're starting to look rubbish

Oh, Dear!
I haven't done this since I was 5

Its always important
To know where the skip is.

Today is the day,
Today is the good one,
Its the day you get your book

I have
So many poems
Illegible…can't understand
A word they say.

By Giorgia Stanza

I remember happiness

I remember happiness
It drifted through my day
On smiles of kids
And clouds
That say
"Hello"

I remember happiness
It seemed to pass my way
In prams of babes
And dads
That say
"Hello"

I remember happiness
It wanted me to play
With words of folk
And stares
That say
"Hello"

By Andrew Newman

Ouch#

I bumped into a man
He said it was okay

But my toe hurts

By Aiden (5 years old)

breath

The wind is cold
The sun is hot
I can build a robot

By Sophie Hunter(8 years old)

After the Beatles

Happiness
      Is a warm bun.

By Chloe Morrish

20 Words

Down, put, stirrup, Danger, recollection, world, mass, poorly, situation, bottom, Imperial Commander,Been, musician, days, garden, published, rolling, stranger, don't, publicappointments(one word typo)

High Queues

17 drunken Scotsmen
waiting for the loo
Is this a high queue?

17 parachutists
waiting to jump out
Another high queue

17 girls
waiting for the boy band to appear
Is this another?

17 men
lining up to greet a friend
Perhaps another one ?

17 scaffolders
Waiting for the foreman
You get the idea

By Simon SD Maclaren

Poemcatcher

Its been a great adventure
And soon will be a book
Of poems I've begged and borrowed
Some stolen, nicked or took
From playful passing strangers
With aspirations high
That their own creations
Others will inspire
To pen a little ditty
A stanza with a rhyme
Release a little happiness
In Soul, in Quake, in Time.

By a grateful PoemCatcher

www.ingramcontent.com/pod-product-compliance
Lightning Source LLC
Chambersburg PA
CBHW050602300426
44112CB00013B/2032